Loving God,

Living Called

A Devotional on the Gospel of Luke

Loving God, Living Called

A Devotional on The Gospel of Luke

By Stephen Cheyney and Cailee Franklin

© 2020 by the authors.

ISBN: 978-0-9889559-2-9

Loving God, Living Called: A Devotional on the Gospel of Luke was created for the students who participate in Niner United. Niner United is the Episcopal, Lutheran, Presbyterian, and United Methodist campus ministry at the University of North Carolina at Charlotte. The campus ministry is united by a common mission: to help students discover abundant life in Jesus Christ by equipping them to live consequential lives of faith. To get connected or support the ministry please visit ninerunited.org.

Contents

Introduction   1

The Life of Jesus

Jesus' Birth   6
Jesus' Baptism   8
Jesus' Temptations   10
Jesus' Rejection   12
Jesus' Transformation   14
Jesus' Entrance   16
Jesus' Arrest   18
Jesus' Death   20
Jesus' Resurrection   22
Jesus' Ascension   24

The Ministry of Jesus

The Compassion of Jesus   32
The Core of Forgiveness   34
The Calming of the Storm   36
The Touch of Jesus   38
The Feeding of the Five Thousand   40
The Reverence of the Storm   42

The Gratitude of the One   44
The Remembrance of the Lord's Supper   46
The Value of Prayer   48
The Presence of God   50

The Message of Jesus

A Lesson about Love   58
A Lesson about Character   60
A Lesson about Discipleship   62
A Lesson about Prayer   64
A Lesson about Hospitality   66
A Lesson about Love   68
A Lesson about Acceptance   70
A Lesson about Humility   72
A Lesson about Attention   74
A Lesson about Persistence   76

The Call of Jesus

Jesus' Call is Personal   84
Jesus' Call is Inclusive   86
Jesus' Call is Uncomfortable   88
Jesus' Call is Challenging   90
Jesus' Call is Liberating   92
Jesus' Call is Costly   94

Jesus' Call is Demanding   96
Jesus' Call is Transformational   98
Jesus' Call is Indispensable   100
Jesus' Call is Irrevocable   102

Helpful Information

About Simon Peter   109
About Food in Luke's Gospel   110
About The New Exodus   111
About The Great Reversal   112
About The Lukan Triangle   113

Introduction

We have titled this devotional Loving God, Living Called. We believe that Luke's gospel reveals the heart of Jesus' relationship with the Father as a God who abundantly loves and calls the Son. We are similarly called to love God. This call comes with great responsibility, especially for our concern of those excluded and left on the margin. The Gospel of Luke paints a masterful portrait of the life of Jesus through compelling storytelling and a vivid narrative. We quickly learn that the Exodus story of Moses provides the basic structure to the life of Jesus. Like in the Moses story, Jesus brought liberation and freedom to the oppressed and believed that God has a redemptive plan for the salvation of all people. Luke extends this through Jesus' call to his disciples and forges the path to a new covenant or new exodus."

Theologians emphasize what they call Luke's great reversal, in which God seems to flip our assumptions, beliefs, and ideas upside down. Jesus afflicted the comfortable and comforted the afflicted. Jesus ate with sinners and didn't give spiritual leaders the time of day. Jesus blessed the poor and warned of the dangers of wealth. Even though the world continues to be male-dominated, Jesus showed favor to the ministry of women. Everything we take for granted for our self-preservation and peace of mind seems to be challenged by the Jesus of Nazareth that Luke presents. Mary's Song, commonly referred to as the Magnificat, exemplifies the great reversal:

"My soul magnifies the Lord,
 and my spirit rejoices in God my Savior,
 for he has looked with favor on the lowliness of his servant.
   Surely, from now on all generations will call me blessed;
for the Mighty One has done great things for me,
   and holy is his name.
His mercy is for those who fear him
   from generation to generation.
He has shown strength with his arm;
   he has scattered the proud in the thoughts of their hearts.
He has brought down the powerful from their thrones,
   and lifted up the lowly;
he has filled the hungry with good things,
   and sent the rich away empty.
He has helped his servant Israel,
   in remembrance of his mercy,
according to the promise he made to our ancestors,
   to Abraham and to his descendants forever."[1]

---

[1] Luke 1:46-55, NRSV

The narrative of Luke's gospel is presented as a quest following Jesus' journey to the cross. Therefore, we have designed this book to be as versatile as possible, so you may also be in a quest to "take up your cross"[2] and follow Jesus. We have divided the gospel into four themes, each consisting of ten sections: The Life of Jesus, The Ministry of Jesus, The Message of Jesus, and The Call of Jesus. We have tried to develop this as a devotional, prayer journal, and guide. We invite you to use this book individually or with groups. You can read it cover to cover, or simply jump to any section and dive in with no prerequisites. As you read Luke, you will notice that Jesus is always on the move in this quest to the cross. We hope that you will use this book as a guide as you travel with him in your own quest for a life with God.

---

[2] Luke 9.23, NRSV

THE LIFE OF JESUS

The Gospel of Luke provides a thorough account of Jesus' life from his birth in chapter two to his ascension in chapter twenty-four. In between, we will cover his baptism, temptation, rejection in his hometown, and his journey into Jerusalem, where he was betrayed, crucified, died, and rose on the third day. Pay close attention, however, to chapter nine where on a mountain's summit, Jesus' face was changed, his clothes became blinding, and his disciples saw him in his glory. Theologians call this Jesus' transfiguration.

In this one story, Luke echoes Jesus' baptism and foreshadows his death and resurrection. Referring to Jesus, a voice from the cloud proclaimed in 9:35, "this is my Son, my Chosen." At this moment, we come to discover that Jesus of Nazareth is more than just a prophet like Moses. He is the Messiah who has come to fulfill the law and prophets and bring about salvation to the entire world!

The voice concluded, listen to him. The life, ministry, message, and call of Jesus continues to speak to us today. Although it is clear that Jesus was transfigured, or transformed that day, the disciples who accompanied him, unfortunately, weren't. The life of Jesus speaks volumes, but we must be ready to listen and witness to his amazement.

Jesus' Birth

In Luke's gospel, the birth of Jesus was preceded by John's birth. There was great anticipation that Mary will be divinely appointed to give birth to Jesus, the Savior. Luke sets the scene in Bethlehem, a humble and unexpected place for God's entry into the world.

Read Luke 2:1-21

What are some things that you already know about the birth of Jesus?

_____

_____

_____

For those who grew up in the church, the story of the birth of Jesus is probably familiar. Each year at Christmastime, churches and towns host live manger scenes with camels and sheep, and sometimes even a real baby that is unknowingly playing the part of Jesus. Yet, the story of Jesus' birth, according to Luke, isn't all that charming or picturesque. It begins with a reminder that the people of Israel were under the Roman Empire's occupation that seized their homeland. So arrogant was the emperor that Luke contends he was registering all of the world. The registration had to take place in one's hometown, so Mary and Joseph went to Bethlehem. While there, Mary gave birth. Considering all of the possible ways the creator of the universe could have made his entry in the world, choosing a poor couple in a humble village is quite odd. Christians celebrate that Jesus is king, so perhaps even stranger is the fact that shepherds were the first to visit the newborn baby. Shepherds lived without homes and were outcasts. Even stranger is that they were led to Jesus by an angel, a messenger of God. Shepherds were so forgotten that the Roman Emperor didn't even find them worthy of being counted for the census. Yet, God sent them the angel, reminding them that they weren't forgotten and were of great worth. The birth of Jesus is God's great reminder that we are also not forgotten and have great worth.

What are some new things that you learned about the birth?

_____

_____

_____

_____

_____

_____

_____

_____

_____

Jesus' Baptism

In the gospel of Mark, John played a significant role in Jesus' baptism. What matters for Luke isn't John, but the role of God. In just two sentences, Luke explains the glory and magnitude of what happened to Jesus in the Jordan.

Read Luke 3:21-22

Have you ever been baptized or seen someone be baptized? If yes, write down some of the details.

_____

_____

_____

Baptism is a Christian sacrament with a significant amount of controversy. While most churches believe baptism is critical to the faith, for thousands of years, churches have argued over its purpose. Luke isn't much help with these theological debates. The writer of the gospel doesn't even record the actual baptism, but instead, he tells us when Jesus was baptized the Holy Spirit descended on him and, in verse 22, a voice from heaven declared, "You are my Son, the Beloved; with you, I am well pleased." In some traditions, the priest or pastor asks the parents of the baby being baptized "what name is he or she given?" Symbolically, the priest then pours water over the baby and calls them by name, as if it were given to them through baptism. Here in Luke's gospel, Jesus isn't named, but he is identified. From this point forward, he will be in ministry to the people as God's son, the Beloved. Jesus' life was incredibly challenging. He was tempted in the wilderness, rejected, accused and ridiculed, arrested, beaten, and killed. For Luke, the baptism itself isn't important, but instead it's what you do with the baptism. Jesus found his identity in the Father, which gave him strength throughout his entire life.

Where do you find your identity and how does it give you strength?

_____

_____

_____

_____

_____

_____

_____

_____

_____

_____

_____

_____

Jesus' Temptations

God's ways are so contrary to ours that they are often opposed. This opposition is what was at stake in the temptation of Jesus. Led out to the wilderness, Jesus was confronted with a choice of whom to follow: God or the world.

Read Luke 4:1-13

In your opinion, what is a temptation?

_____

_____

_____

The temptation of Jesus is one of the most obscure stories found in Luke's gospel. The Spirit leads Jesus into the wilderness of testing by the devil for forty days. This concept alone consumes much of the early church's time. It considers deep philosophical questions like what is the relationship between Jesus and the Holy Spirit, who is the devil, and who is God? The story, though, continues with the actual content of the test, or the temptations. Jesus was tempted to have complete authority over life (having food to live by), over the world (having power and wealth), and over the soul (to protect the temple in Jerusalem). The more you consider the temptations, the less harmful they look.

After all, Jesus is the ultimate authority, and each of these causes has merit. An in-depth read will find that the devil is less atrocious than we might first think. And that's Luke's point! While these are great causes, Jesus' loyalty was in God's will alone. Similarly, we also have choices on where to place our loyalties. Some people choose personal pleasure over wealth. Some choose wealth over allegiance to their country. Some choose allegiance of their country over loyalty to their church. Some choose dedication to their church over faith in God. Like Jesus, we all have choices that seem honorable. Jesus chose service to God.

What are some of your temptations?

_____

_____

_____

_____

_____

Where are you choosing to place your loyalty?

_____

_____

_____

_____

Jesus' Rejection

After being tempted in the wilderness for forty days and nights, Jesus returned to Galilee. He remained in Galilee throughout the gospel while teaching and healing. On one occasion, Jesus was teaching in his hometown of Nazareth. There he encountered opposition.

Read Luke 4:16-30

Who is someone that you're not happy with right now, maybe even mad at? Why?

_____

_____

_____

Jesus often taught in the temple or synagogue. Much like you would see in a church service, one day in his hometown of Nazareth, Jesus stood up to read from the prophet Isaiah. He read to the crowd, Isaiah 61:1-2, that begin, "The Spirit of the Sovereign Lord is on me." Unlike what you would hear in church, Jesus personified the scripture, reading it as if it were speaking about himself. Then he rolled it up, sat down, and said, the scripture had been fulfilled. Jesus was, in essence, letting everyone in the place know that he was the anointed one that the prophet Isaiah promised. It was a first-century mic drop. Luke stated when they heard this, all in the synagogue were filled with rage. Because of this, they threw Jesus out and ran him to the side of a mountain where they could throw him off. Jesus escaped, never to return to Nazareth. They were only mad at what Jesus had said, not done. But why? Up to this point, Luke hadn't recorded any of Jesus healings or miracles. He was just reading from the scriptures and proclaiming good news. Except, the good news wasn't just for those in the synagogue. Instead, the good news is for everyone.

Depending on the situation, anger can be either positive or negative. These leaders had excessive negative anger at Jesus for including others. What are some good, Christ-like things that you can (or should) do, that may anger others?

_____

_____

_____

_____

_____

_____

_____

_____

Jesus' Transformation

Luke presents several chapters of Jesus' ministry of healings and teachings. His transformation experience on the mountaintop was confirmation that his ministry was aligned with the Father's work.

Read Luke 9:28-36

Give an example of how your day was completely altered in the past.

_____

_____

_____

Have you ever been at a restaurant, having a great conversation with friends, and then someone new shows up, and everything changes? Having the extra person simply changes the entire dynamic. Even though the change may be good, we are often hesitant about change because it often alters our comfort level. One slight shift or modification can make a huge impact. One friend may be the cause of a significant amount of toxicity in your life. One incident or accident may have set you on a path that you regret or distresses you. One broken promise, one missed assignment, or one bad day can make a tremendous difference. This is how transformation works. It also works in the reverse patten. One last-minute decision to go to an event could lead you to meet your life's love. Clicking submit could start your journey to grad school. Luke tells us that Jesus and three disciples went to the mountain to pray. There they encountered an incredible and mysterious spiritual moment. Most Bibles call what happened on the mountaintop, the transfiguration, or transformation, of Jesus. Up to this point, Jesus was living out his identity as God's blessed son through temptation and rejection. Now, that day on the mountaintop, Jesus' divinity was solidified, and he would forever be changed. Yet, it many ways, the change was a choice. Jesus was open to being changed. The three disciples who were with him did not change at all. Maybe they were not open to the change or were not able to understand what was happening, which inhibited them from being changed. If we cannot understand the circumstances, it can be impossible to accept and be open to any change.

Take some time to reflect on how you deal with change. Are you open to change? What could you miss out on if you're not open to change?

_____

_____

_____

_____

_____

_____

Jesus' Entrance

In Luke 9:51, Luke says Jesus "set his face to go to Jerusalem." Ten chapters later, Jesus finally arrived. At that point, he had a following, and there was a lot on the line.

Read Luke 19:28-40

Have you ever seen a parade? When and where was it? Who was at the end of the parade?

_____

_____

_____

Since his baptism in chapter three, Jesus has been journeying toward Jerusalem, the most important city in the biblical world. From its beginning, Jerusalem has been the obsession of countless empires and tyrants. Rising from valleys that surround it, it wasn't unusual for royal processions that could be seen for miles to parade into the city, as a sign of authority and control. During the Passover, it was likely that Pilate, the governor, entered the city on the same day as Jesus. The Roman rulers probably came from the north or west, and Jesus came from the east, at the Mount of Olives. But Jesus' procession was far from ordinary. After all, he chose a simple, unimposing donkey as his ride. Yet, what was ordinary for Jesus? One can easily imagine that his parade may have included all of the misfits that he encountered throughout his journey. If so, this parade would have been a disorganized, messy, and wild collection of society's undesirables, following the one true freedom-giver, Jesus. Typical to Luke's gospel, it seems whom we follow is a choice. We can either grasp onto what is trending, what gives us pleasure, or power. Alternatively, we can join the less popular caravan that embarrassingly includes everyone and shouts blessed is the king who comes in the name of the Lord!

What are some things that you follow and why do you follow them?

_____

_____

_____

_____

_____

_____

_____

_____

_____

_____

Jesus' Arrest

Jesus' ministry in Jerusalem continued, despite the opposition. He had been betrayed by one of his own, and the power-hungry religious leaders were out to destroy him and his message.

Read Luke 22:47-53

Describe a situation when you felt betrayed.

_____

_____

_____

After Jesus entered into Jerusalem for the Passover, he conflicted with the religious leaders by cleansing the temple and by stirring up controversy, his authority was questioned, his disciple Judas betrayed him, and he celebrated the Passover meal. We pick up the story after the meal ended, where Jesus and his disciples were praying at the Mount of Olives. It was the moment of truth. From the serenity of prayer and meditation, Judas violently breaks into the scene, leading a group to arrest Jesus. The disciples would have none of this. Their guts led them to a quick response. They felt they had to defend their friend Jesus. So with an intense swing of a sword, savagery begins. Just like that, one of Jesus' disciples cut someone's ear right off their head. These disciples were Jewish. They were familiar with the Levitical law eye for eye, tooth for tooth. Maybe they figured ear for ear was okay? They had good intentions. Because they loved Jesus so much, they felt obligated to protect him. We might not sever someone's ear, but we sometimes go to great lengths to stand up for what we believe. We justify our actions. We defend our pride and property. For example, some Americans have rights they want to protect, so they take up arms and stand their ground. Yet, to all of this, in verse 51, Jesus clearly said, "No more of this!" Jesus was tired of the way things were. The ways of the world are simply not the ways of God. Violence, retribution, revenge, payback, and force simply have no place in Jesus' kingdom.

When have you let violence or revenge take over a situation? How can you follow Jesus' words and no longer allow these actions to be acceptable?

_____

_____

_____

_____

_____

_____

_____

_____

Jesus' Death

Jesus died at the hands of the Roman Empire and the autocratic religious authority. Jesus' death is a theological perplexity, as we now must consider what it means to confess our faith in a crucified man.

Read Luke 23:26-49

What are your thoughts after reading this passage?

_____

_____

_____

The death of Jesus may consume more theological pages than any religious concept. Raymond Brown's book *Death of the Messiah* is 877 pages. Fleming Rutledge's book *The Crucifixion* is 696 pages. These are just two examples of thousands of books that attempt to understand what happened to Jesus at what Luke calls the place of the skull. The truth is, we will never fully grasp the significance of Jesus' death. Thankfully, Luke gives us three clues to help us remain hopeful, even in the worst situations. First, even at the cross, Jesus continues to teach us. Jesus urged his followers to switch their sadness about his forthcoming death to being concerned for the fate of their city. Second, is the realization that nothing, not even crucifixion, stops Jesus from his love for us. In his last breaths, Jesus prayed for forgiveness for the criminals hung beside him. This had to have assured the Apostle Paul when he wrote not even death can separate us from the love of God (Romans 8:38-39). Finally, Jesus remains in prayer with the Father, as he commends his spirit and breathes his last. Jesus never wavered from teaching us, loving us, and living into his vocation as God's son.

Which one of the three clues helps you remain hopeful? What about this clue is comforting for you right now?

_____

_____

_____

_____

_____

_____

_____

_____

_____

_____

_____

_____

Jesus' Resurrection

Death cannot stop God. Jesus' resurrection was the fulfillment of God's promise to liberate his people. The promise was embodied in the life, teachings, healings, and death of Jesus. Yet, the promise was and is still today, ultimately ratified with God's victory over death.

Read Luke 24:1-12

When was a time you weren't believed even though you felt you were right?

_____

_____

_____

The resurrection of Jesus is remarkable; it may be the most essential element of the entire scripture. God, through Jesus' resurrection, proves that death is defeated. Perhaps just as important is our responsibility to share this incredible act of God with the world. The women in this story tried to share what happened, but no one believed them. Maybe they didn't believe them because it was such a complicated situation and hard to grasp fully, or perhaps they didn't believe them because they were women. These women played a unique role in Jesus' life, though. They were present at events and always listened to and followed Jesus. They were at the crucifixion and were on the way to anoint his body. It is clear that these women were close listeners and followers of Jesus because they could remember what he said and comprehend what had happened. Even though they were dismissed, they had every reason to be considered reputable sources. Sometimes we may have knowledge on a particular subject but are dismissed because our audience isn't fully able to understand at that time, or we are dismissed because of who we are. The same is true for this situation. We must remember not to get discouraged if others are not ready to hear. These women rightly discerned a responsibility to proclaim the good news, despite the obstacles, just as we should.

How can you be like these women and not get discouraged despite obstacles you may encounter? What is one specific situation you can apply this to?

_____

_____

_____

_____

_____

_____

_____

_____

Jesus' Ascension

In the gospel, Luke shares the beginning of Jesus' ministry with a very brief baptismal description. Now he ends the entire account with a very brief report of Jesus' ascension to heaven. More so, the gospel itself begins and ends in the temple.

Read Luke 24:50-53

To ascend means to rise up. Name a time when you have risen to the occasion.

_____

_____

_____

Every story needs a good ending, even if the story is unresolved. In many ways, this describes the ascension of Jesus. He was presented in the temple as the anointed king of Israel, and as the one prophesied to release the oppressed from their bondage, give good news to the poor, and heal the sick. Jesus preached and taught in the villages, encountered opposition, and developed a group of disciples who followed him to Jerusalem. In his vocation as God's son, he widened the kingdom to include everyone, he suffered and died on the cross, only to be raised the third day. After his return, he encountered strangers and friends alike and finally ascended to heaven. Yet, why? It seems incredibly unresolved unless Luke wanted to begin and end the gospel in the same tone. The tone, of course, is that of hope. In the beginning, in the occupied and impoverished land of ancient Palestine, there was hope that something new can happen. There was hope that God was at work in the world and would bring blessings and good news to those who were rejected and suffering. And now at the end - and even today - there is hope. There is hope that God is still at work and continues to bless us, especially those who are denied the essence of human dignity, those who are sick and suffering, and those who are destitute. There is hope, because Jesus blesses them in Bethany, and continues to bless us here. And, since we have been so greatly blessed, we must live our lives as a blessing to others.

What are some examples of when you have seen how God is still at work in you and in the world today?

_____

_____

_____

_____

_____

_____

_____

Notes & Journaling

The Ministry of Jesus

In the middle of the gospel, just after Jesus healed a boy, Luke wrote in 9:48 that Jesus took aside a child and said, "Whoever welcomes this child in my name welcomes me, and whoever welcomes me welcomes the one who sent me; for the least among all of you is the greatest." This one verse is an excellent summary of Jesus' ministry. As we journey through his ministry, we will witness the healing and compassionate side of Jesus, who cares and gives new life to even the least among us.

In one story, Jesus encounters ten lepers. They were social outcasts, considered vile, inferior, and dangerous. It's sad that since the beginning of time, we have continually marginalized certain people. Jesus, however, didn't find their leprosy disgraceful. Jesus actually defended the plight of every outsider. What's shameful, though, is that we belittle anyone, for all of us are equally children of God. In this story, Jesus healed all ten, but only one showed gratitude. It's unspoken, yet undeniable that this one recognized that what Jesus did was a marvelous act of God giving him a new life.

In each case, we will discover God's marvelous and astonishing acts in the ministry of Jesus. Jesus' ministry is so incredible that, like this one leper, we maybe should fall on our faces and thank him. In every story we highlight, you will see that the ministry of Jesus demands a response. The Pharisees and religious leaders in Luke's gospel rejected Jesus, but our response should be like that of the leper, fully glorifying God. The healings and miracles matter. Yet, what matters most is how we respond to Jesus' invitation to new life.

The Compassion of Jesus

Jesus was traveling south from Capernaum, where he entered Nain, a town not far from his hometown of Nazareth. There Jesus encountered a funeral procession. Luke says a mother's only son had died. Jesus saw the mother and had compassion.

Read Luke 7:11-17

Do you typically hold your emotions in or prefer to talk about them with everyone?

_____

_____

_____

Unfortunately, death is common. Almost every day we experience or hear about death. Sometimes we read about it in the news, and sometimes it personally affects us. It hit really close to home for the mother in this passage. Luke tells us she was a widow and had just lost her only son. The grief she was experiencing must have been unbelievable. When we grieve or find ourselves in desperate situations, we may call out to God or others for help. Other times we may keep our feelings to ourselves, sometimes a little too often. Even when we face tragedy, loss, or pain, we try to hide being seen as an emotional wreck. However, we are still seen when we are faking and trying to hold everything in. We can't even hide from God. This mother didn't approach Jesus, yet he saw her and had compassion for her. The text could be translated that he had a deep, gut-wrenching compassion for her. He saw her emotional state and knew how hard her life was going to be moving forward. So Jesus simply touched the casket, and the dead man came to life. The story of the raising the widow's son is a foreshadowing of Jesus' most compassionate miracle, the resurrection. Scholars link Jesus' compassion for her to his identity as the Messiah. In essence, Jesus was showing the genuine character of God. God sees us, in all of our circumstances, and has gut-wrenching compassion.

When has there been a time that you felt seen by God?

_____

_____

_____

_____

_____

_____

_____

_____

_____

The Core of Forgiveness

Jesus found himself once again at a dinner. In this passage, two people are highlighted. The first is a sinful woman who anointed Jesus with oil from a jar and her tears. The second is a Pharisee named Simon. Simon called this woman a sinner, whereas Jesus called her forgiven.

Read Luke 7:36-50

Be real. When's the last time you judged someone? Go ahead and name it...

_____

_____

_____

Simon was both a member of the elite religious establishment (he is a Pharisee) and someone who had the means to host a dinner party. Nicer homes often had large courtyards where members of the community could enter and eat from the leftover food if not welcomed to the banquet. The woman in this story was clearly not invited. Simon, in disgust, simply called her a sinner. Unfortunately, sometimes we also see people as sinners. We may not use that word, but we pass judgment. Even at the best of times when we are trying to be gracious, we can catch ourselves thinking or saying disparaging things about others. Often, we also see ourselves this way. Many Christians were brought up in churches that emphasized our human sinfulness. We've had it preached and drilled into our brains that we are sinners, which sometimes makes it difficult to see ourselves as a child of God. We get caught in a trap. We either easily think less of others, less of ourselves, or both. It's interesting that before Jesus saw any sin, he saw a woman who was generously giving him praise. Jesus was blunt. He directly asked Simon if he saw her. In other words, do you see her as a sinner, or as a person? No matter our sin, public or private, we are people first. There is value in our humanity. We were created in God's image for good. Jesus commended the woman's love and forgave her instead of condemning her.

We all pass judgement on others, and ourselves. Make two lists:

What I Need to Forgive Myself For	What I Need to Forgive Others For

The Calming of the Storm

Jesus' disciples were fishermen, so it was probably routine for them to travel by boat across the lake. At this point, large crowds followed Jesus, and the boat also served as a place of refuge and rest. That particular day, a violent storm frightened the disciples while Jesus slept.

Read Luke 8:22-25

What is a storm in your life that you have recently been dealing with?

_____

_____

_____

The lake Jesus and his disciples were on is also known as the Sea of Galilee. Most days, the lake is still and peaceful. It is a beautiful setting, with a consistently mild climate, and ideal for recreation and fishing. However, the nearby hills create a valley that allow strong winds from the Mediterranean Sea to reach the lake. These winds produce intense and violent storms that catch even the most seasoned fishermen unaware. It's in one of these storms the disciples and Jesus found themselves in. The boat started to take on water, and they were about to capsize. You don't have to be a boater to understand the surprise of chaos. One day things are going well, and the next all hell breaks loose. Throughout life, we will face various forces out of our control. Sudden illness, accidents, the loss of jobs, parents getting divorced, and the death of a loved one are all types of chaos that can test our faith. Frightened, the disciples woke Jesus and cried out. Waking, he responded in verse 25, "Where is your faith?" In similar circumstances, Jesus might ask us the same. Notice, Jesus didn't rebuke them for losing their faith. Instead, Jesus was asking them to look for the faith they already had. In essence, Jesus being in the boat with them was faith enough. God is still with us, even in the storms of our lives. So when the winds whip up and chaos ensues, Jesus isn't questioning our faith - he's calling on us to remember his presence with us. In this case, Jesus calmed the storm. God still acts today to calm the storms in our lives.

How have you seen God calm your storm or parts of your storm recently?

_____

_____

_____

_____

_____

_____

_____

The Touch of Jesus

This story is about a young girl who had just died. The story is sandwiched with another story of a woman who sought out Jesus in the crowd. She touched Jesus. He asked who touched him, and everyone around him denied it. Despite the denials, Jesus insisted he had been touched.

Read Luke 8:40-56

When is a time that you have felt like an outcast, an outsider, or excluded from your group or community?

_____

_____

_____

It was probably pretty easy to remember a time that you felt left out or excluded. During these times, it is common to feel lonely and hurt, especially when it wasn't your choice to not join the group. That's probably how this woman felt after twelve years of isolation from her community. The Jewish law called for her to be secluded from everyone until she stopped bleeding because if she touched anyone, she would make them impure. The same is true for the girl who had just died. According to Jewish law, whoever touched the corpse would also be impure. Regardless of the laws, Jesus allowed himself to be touched by the woman, and he touched the girl's hand. This physical touch allowed both of them to be included in their communities again. Today we don't get a physical touch from Jesus, but instead, maybe we get an invitation to join a community that is inclusive and welcoming. Or perhaps a friend reminds us that we are important and loved. At some point, we all need that touch and, therefore, need to be that touch for someone else.

List three ways you can be like the touch of Jesus for someone else.

1.

2.

3.

The Feeding of the Five Thousand

The crowds followed Jesus and his disciples to Bethsaida. As the day drew to an end, the disciples asked Jesus to send the crowd away so that they could eat. Instead, Jesus told the disciples to feed them. The disciples were perplexed on how to do this without any food.

Read Luke 9:10-17

What are some things that you have done to help those who hunger?

_____

_____

_____

Jesus feeding the five thousand could be one of the most well-known biblical stories. It's the only miracle of Jesus that's found in all four gospels. In Luke's gospel, it has a liturgical or worship-like element as Jesus takes, blesses, breaks, and gives the food. These four verbs are also found in Luke's Emmaus road story (Luke 24) and the last supper story (Luke 22). Notably different from the rest of the gospels, Luke tells us they were in a deserted place. Deserted didn't mean unpopulated. Luke tells us there were about five thousand men there. Imagine how many more if he had estimated the women and children!

It was deserted because there was no food. This shows that food deserts are not new. Just think: the problem of world hunger is so pervasive that it even affected Jesus. Even so, the disciples of Jesus (called apostles in this passage) knew where to find food. The availability of food was never an issue and, ironically, isn't an issue today. The earth produces enough food for everyone. Just think about how much food we waste. Equitable distribution of food, however, was the issue. The food wasn't available for this crowd. Considering how much time Jesus spent with the poor, outcast, and marginalized, it seems things haven't changed too much. So, Jesus figured a way to feed everyone. Today, we are still recipients of God's abundance, as the Holy Spirit continues to feed us spiritually. More so, just as Jesus instructed the disciples to feed the crowd, God continues to feed the physically hungry through us.

If Jesus continues to ask his disciples to feed the hungry, what steps can you take to follow his instruction?

_____

_____

_____

_____

_____

_____

_____

The Reverence of the Sabbath

Throughout Luke's gospel, we find Jesus in the synagogue, the Jewish house of worship. This particular sabbath day, while in the synagogue, Jesus encountered a woman who been disabled for eighteen years.

Read Luke 13:10-17

Who are some heroes that you admire?

_____

_____

_____

We often see stories on social media or the news about heroes. These are the people who risk their life to pull someone from a burning car or jump from a bridge to save a drowning victim. We are also familiar with the term everyday hero that gives credit to teachers, nurses, bus drivers, electrical linemen, and others who sacrifice significantly for others' service. Often, those whom we call heroes have to break the rules or laws to achieve their goals. For example, protesters may stay a night in jail as an act of civil disobedience to change or bring attention to antiquated or unjust laws. Rules and laws change over time. Sometimes we outlive the need for a particular law, sometimes the law was created with ill intent, and sometimes we simply abuse the law to suppress others' rights. Remembering the sabbath was one of the Ten Commandments found in the Torah. The purpose of the sabbath is to rest. However, over time the law became expanded and more complex. Unfortunately, the more complicated something is, the more prone it is to misinterpretation or misuse. In this passage, Jesus heals a woman on the sabbath. Faced with such a great need, Jesus decided to break the sabbath law. Jesus continues to ask us to put people first. People over property, people over law, and people over the sabbath. Jesus even called the woman he healed free. Jesus frees us from the burdens of life, even if the burden is religion.

List some other occasions when the need is greater than the rules or laws that prevent the needs from being resolved.

-

-

-

The Gratitude of the One

Jesus stopped in numerous villages on his way to Jerusalem. In this passage, Jesus was approached, from a distance, by ten men who were sick. They called on Jesus to show mercy and heal them.

Read Luke 17:11-19

What surprised you in this passage?

_____

_____

_____

Luke, and the other gospels, record many of Jesus' healings. Some Christians believe these healings were literal occurrences, while others believe they were metaphorical. This begs the question, what does it mean to be healed? If someone conquers a fatal disease or escapes a horrific accident, is this a healing? Any way you address it, healings are subjective. The subjectivity intensifies when we find ourselves in situations when things don't work out the way we desire. We might wonder why God didn't heal. In this passage, ten lepers were healed. Surprisingly, only the outsider took the time to acknowledge and express gratitude for his healing. Somehow the other nine didn't recognize what happened. Ninety percent of them overlooked the healing, while ten percent focused on it. This could be happening in our lives regularly. God may always heal, but we only acknowledge it, maybe ten percent of the time. Therefore, it seems that God's healing nature isn't under review, but rather our perception. We don't want to only focus on ten percent and let the rest fade away. We should wish to acknowledge and express gratitude for all one hundred percent. This story stretches us to widen our view and give God thanks for the changes, transformations, and even coincidences in our lives.

Name some times that you have recently seen changes, transformations, or coincidences that you could thank God for.

_____

_____

_____

_____

_____

_____

_____

_____

_____

The Remembrance of the Lord's Supper

Religious pilgrims traveled to Jerusalem every year to celebrate the Passover, commemorating God's deliverance of the Israelites from the slavery of Egypt. On the first, and sometimes the second night of the Passover, participants would celebrate the seder, a ritual with storytelling, songs, food, and wine.

Read Luke 22:14-23

What comes to mind when you think of communion?

_____

_____

_____

Just before Jesus was arrested, he dined with his disciples one last time in what we have come to call the Lord's Supper or the Last Supper. We remember this today by celebrating communion in church. Communion simply indicates the presence of a community. Sometimes it is also called the Eucharist, derived from the Greek word *eucharistia*, which means thanks. The meal is a blessing of sorts, which is fitting because the Greek word *eucharistia* is a translation of the Hebrew word *berekah*, which means blessing. We recall this meal by celebrating it often because Jesus said to do this in remembrance of him.

Interestingly when Jesus and his disciples were dining that evening, they also remembered the Passover meal, found in the Torah. Repeating something over and over is a practice. Practice makes habit, and habit changes lifestyle. We need to be aware that habits can also become routine and empty. Sometimes when we focus on communion, all we see is the empty, repetitive, routine. We need to remember that what's out of focus is holy and sacred. Like when we take a picture in portrait mode, we often pay attention to only the things right in front of us. This myopia makes much of life fuzzy and unclear. We celebrate communion not because we feel holy or sacred, and not because we even understand it clearly. Instead, we celebrate it because Jesus asks us to remember him. With practice, the hope is that the holy and sacred will become less fuzzy and more clear.

What are some things about communion that you wish were more clear?

_____

_____

_____

_____

_____

_____

_____

_____

The Value of Prayer

In Luke 21, we learn that Jesus spent his days in the temple teaching and his nights at the Mount of Olives during the Passover celebration. In this passage, Luke gives us a window into the intimate prayer life of Jesus.

Read Luke 22:39-46

How do you usually cope when you're going through a tough time?

_____

_____

_____

We will inevitably experience rough and hard times throughout our life. At some point, we will all experience a loss that completely changes and disrupts our world. Some circumstances may provide you with time to prepare for the loss, and others will unexpectedly blindside you. Either way, it still hurts. The disciples were preparing for a hard time that could end in loss. Instead of listening to Jesus' commands to pray, they slept. They weren't sleeping because it was late, and they wanted to get enough rest; they were sleeping because they were physically and mentally exhausted. Grief and sorrow can drain you. Jesus was also preparing for a difficult time, but instead, he chose to pray. This was not an unusual occurrence, though. Throughout Luke's gospel, it is evident that Jesus had a consistent prayer life. He prayed during the good, the bad, and the everyday, or the boring. Jesus used prayer as a foundation for strength throughout his lifetime, so it should be no surprise that he especially prayed during this time. Jesus was clear in his command to the disciples to pray, and they failed, just like we often do. Sometimes it feels like too much time or energy to pray. Sometimes the feeling of exhaustion, or other distractions, take priority instead of praying. Other times we fail to pray because we choose to try and handle our emotions and feelings instead of taking them to God. Even though it is comforting knowing the disciples dealt with their sorrow as we do, we should try to handle it as Jesus did. We should strive to follow Jesus' model and integrate prayer as a foundation in our daily life. After all, God is always listening in the good, the bad, and the boring.

Reflect on your current prayer life.

_____

_____

_____

_____

_____

_____

_____

The Presence of God

On the day Jesus rose from the dead, two disciples walked and talked about what had just happened. A stranger joined them and started to explain to him everything they had just experienced. Even though they were convinced they knew the entire story of Jesus, they didn't realize that he was the stranger walking with them.

Read Luke 24:13-35

Name some occasions that you realized God's presence, only after the fact.

_____

_____

_____

In a matter of days, the people who followed Jesus were thrust into a whirlwind of emotions. Their friend, who they came to know as God's son, was arrested, tortured, and killed. As wild as this seems, reports were now flowing that this same Jesus escaped death by rising to life. What Christians celebrate on Easter, that Christ is risen, was unimaginable days after his death. So, word spread, and everyone was in disbelief, including these two men walking to the village of Emmaus. Luke lets the reader know right away that Jesus started to walk with these men. Yet, in failing to recognize Jesus, they filled him in as if he were unaware. It's intriguing that Jesus played along, and let them tell him everything. He never stopped, interrupted, or corrected them. Instead, Jesus attentively listened with patience and interest. The same remains true today. Jesus never forces himself on us. Our decision to believe and follow Jesus is always our decision, but he will always meet you where you are. He met these men where they were even though they had no clue they were walking with him. Maybe we should ask ourselves, how do we recognize Jesus today? One thing we can know from this story is that Jesus will always join us. He will be with us in the ordinary everyday routine, on our way to class, hanging out with friends, and even when we eat. So when it feels like he isn't there, remember to take the time to recognize him, because he is there.

How can you more intentionally recognize the presence of God?

_____

_____

_____

_____

_____

_____

_____

_____

Notes & Journaling

_____
_____
_____
_____
_____
_____
_____
_____
_____
_____
_____
_____
_____
_____
_____
_____
_____
_____
_____
_____

THE MESSAGE OF JESUS

In the Gospel of Luke, Jesus has a lot to teach us. One of Jesus' most prevalent teaching styles is his use of parables. Parables are fable-like allegories that reveal a plethora of truths and can never really be solved or finished. In an attempt to define what a parable is, Harvard professor and New Testament scholar, George Buttrick, wrote, "the old definition, 'an earthly story with a heavenly meaning,' can hardly be improved."[3] We believe his definition stands strong today.

---

[3] Steven J. Voris. Preaching Parables: A Metaphorical Interfaith Approach. Paulist Press, 2008, 3.

Jesus used parables throughout his life and ministry. Luke records Jesus saying more than twenty parables, most of them unique to Luke. Since Jesus always seemed to use parables, it isn't wrong to view his life as a parable. Through Jesus, we are provided such an amazing picture of who God is, but once we think we've figured it out, we again are surprised. So, keep this in mind: Jesus will surprise you.

Although Jesus loved them, he didn't always speak in parables. Nonetheless, in everything he did, Jesus was teaching. Therefore, we have also included ways Jesus teaches us in addition to his parables. Part of the life of discipleship is discerning Jesus' message, so, still look for what might surprise you, as Jesus teaches us about God's will and dream for our lives.

A Lesson about Love

After selecting the twelve to be his disciples, Jesus preached to the crowds. With a set of four blessings, Jesus explained what scholars call the great reversal.

Read Luke 6:20-36

What do you think is the theme of this passage?

_____

_____

_____

Those familiar with the Bible may recall Jesus' sermon on the mount in Matthew's gospel. Luke has a parallel account that some call the sermon on the plain. Here in Luke's gospel, Jesus teaches to the crowd from a level plain (so not from a mountain), and while there are similarities between the two gospels, it is essential to distance the two and give Luke's account the attention it deserves. The most striking difference is Luke's detail of Jesus' insistence on God's preferential treatment of the poor. There is no room for sentimentality here. Jesus doesn't say "blessed are the poor in spirit" like he does in Matthew 5:3. In Luke, the poverty of concern is economic. The hunger in the discussion isn't spiritual hunger; it's the lack of food. The joy and laughing invoked in Jesus' sermon aren't from celebrating with friends, but instead refers to the sheer delight oppressors sense when they benefit from others' suffering. In Luke's gospel, Jesus is direct. God's blessings are for those who have been excluded, rejected, and defamed. However, the blessed aren't off the hook. In verse 27, Jesus continues to teach all of us to "Love your enemies, do good to those who hate you, bless those who curse you, pray for those who abuse you." Jesus isn't establishing a victim-victimizer relationship. He never says accept those who curse you. He never calls for us to tolerate abuse. Blessings, however, do come with responsibilities. Jesus calls us to forgive and show kindness. A life with God calls us away from excess and vindictiveness and toward love.

Who do you need to forgive and show kindness? How can you move away from excess and vindictiveness in your daily life?

_____

_____

_____

_____

_____

_____

_____

A Lesson about Character

In his sermon on the plain, Jesus instructed the crowd (and us) to abstain from judging others, grow fruitfully, and care for the inner core and foundational integrity of our faith.

Read Luke 6:37-49

Why do you think it is sometimes so easy to judge others?

_____

_____

_____

There is a lot to unpack in what Jesus says in each of these passages. At first glance, it seems like there are many suggestions on what to do and what not to do. But, they each promote self-reflection on ways to be the person God calls us to be. Every single person is flawed in many different ways. So when we choose to judge others on their flaws, it is almost like we forget about ours or think theirs are worse. In reality, if we took the time to reflect honestly, we would realize that we have no room to judge or compare ourselves to anyone else. After all, comparing does not allow us to grow. Like a tree and its fruit, we must grow in a healthy way to produce good products. The fruit comes directly from the tree, and what we say, what we do, and who we are comes directly from our hearts. If the fruit tastes or looks bad, one might assume any fruit that comes from the tree is bad. If we negatively present ourselves, others might think that our heart and our intentions are also bad. Even if we are faithful in trying to produce good fruit, we will encounter storms that can wreck everything. This is why it's so important to make sure our foundation is solid. To build this secure foundation, we must first listen and then act accordingly. If we only listen and do not act, or if we do not pay attention, things may seem and look good until a storm comes and destroys anything and everything. We need a solid foundation so that we can produce good fruit and be critically aware of ourselves. Without it, we may get trapped in a constant cycle of judging others and only producing negatived and rotten fruit.

Take some time to reflect. What kind of foundation do you have and what kind of fruit are you producing? What needs to be changed and how will you do it?

_____

_____

_____

_____

_____

_____

_____

A Lesson about Discipleship

In one of the most recited parables, found only in Luke's gospel, Jesus noted that the most unlikely person springs to action and ends up being the hero. This critique on religious inaction is followed by an encounter Jesus had with two women that emphasized how a disciple's role also includes listening.

Read Luke 10:25-42

Are you someone who is more likely going to do or going to listen?

_____

_____

_____

It may seem unlikely to put the Parable of the Good Samaritan and the story of Mary and Martha together, but they both teach us similar things. In the parable, a lawyer was reminded to love God wholeheartedly and to love his neighbor as himself. There was a deep hatred between the Jews and the Samaritans, so to this Jewish lawyer, a Samaritan would be the least likely person to show love and compassion to a Jew in great need. The lawyer was great at debating and had the knowledge to answer all of Jesus' questions, but he was told to go and do, not just to listen. Likewise, Mary was intently listening to Jesus. Martha was frustrated because she was not doing what she was supposed to do. This time, Jesus tells Martha not to be so busy doing things and to take time to listen and learn. Through these stories, we can see that there is a time where we should go and do, and there is a time where we should sit and listen. The tricky part is knowing when we should do which one. Both of these circumstances will apply to us in different situations, so we must take the time to discern if it is a time to do or a time to sit. We must also make sure that we are not too preoccupied with what we think we should do that we miss out on what is really important in that moment.

Times I should have done more	Times I should have listened more

A Lesson about Prayer

Jesus' prayer-life is a major theme of Luke's gospel. Witnessing this first hand, one of his disciples asked Jesus to teach them the finer points of prayer. Jesus obliged and offered them the gold standard.

Read Luke 11:1-13

How did you learn how to pray?

_____

_____

_____

Jesus began his instruction on prayer to the disciples by addressing the prayer to the Father, who is hallowed. Today we might say holy or divine. It's not surprising that Jesus puts the spotlight on his intimate relationship with God. What is shocking is that Jesus proclaims God is both holy and approachable. Until Jesus' birth and life, religious people only considered God holy, never intimately. Having a personal relationship with God is paramount to our faith. We pray to the Father who personally knows our name, loves us, and seeks to relate to us. God is holy and reverent, the creator, sustainer, and redeemer. God is also our friend in confidant. Jesus even continued and said in verse 9, "Ask, and it will be given you; search, and you will find; knock, and the door will be opened for you." However, before Jesus said this to his disciples, he reminded them that living a godly life isn't only about our relationship with God. Our relationship with the world, our community, and our neighbors is equally important. Give us each day our daily bread is a communal request. Forgive us our sins is likewise. We are indebted to one another and, thus, people who pray to the Father, have an obligation to feed, forgive, and protect others from their times of trial. The Lord's Prayer draws attention to the fact that we need God and each other.

Write down the version of The Lord's prayer that you recite. Take some time to reflect on how it shows the importance of our relationship with God and others.

_____

_____

_____

_____

_____

_____

_____

_____

_____

A Lesson about Hospitality

This parable emphasizes our attitude when we are status-minded. Eugene Peterson sums it up as, "If you walk around with your nose in the air, you're going to end up flat on your face (Luke 14:11, MSG)."

Read Luke 14:1-14

What does the word hospitality mean to you?

_____

_____

_____

No one wants to feel shame or embarrassed. It was true when Jesus was giving this advice, and it is still true today. Shame is the sense of feeling undeserving or unworthy, as if we're imposters. Everyone wants to feel valued, and even honored and special on occasion. It seems outrageous, but this story reminds us that humility invites the opportunity to feel honor instead of shame. According to Jesus, we do this by showing hospitality. From the root word host, it makes sense to welcome our friends. But, hospitality also means to welcome a wider circle, specifically those who are hostile toward us. In this sense, it can mean anyone outside your typical social circle. Hospitality is about welcoming everyone, especially those who may not even have a group to welcome you to in return. We should not invite those outside of our group because we think we have to. Instead, it should be genuine. Besides, showing hospitality out of reluctance would only exacerbate the guest's sense of shame. Also, people aren't projects. We should never treat anyone like they are a piece of work that we are trying to change. Jesus chose to be around those outside his inner circle because he saw the image of God within them. Jesus saw their worth and sees ours. It's time for us to do the same.

What are some ways that you can be more hospitable to others?

_____

_____

_____

_____

_____

_____

_____

_____

_____

_____

_____

_____

A Lesson about Value

Jesus provided a trio of parables (the lost sheep and coin here, and the lost son in our next devotion) that reveal the lengths at which God will go to seek the lost and alienated. All the more, when God finds the lost, celebration ensues.

Read Luke 15:1-10

What is something you have lost that you searched for endlessly? What were your emotions when you found or couldn't find it?

_____

_____

_____

Both of these parables feature someone who lost something and refuses to give up until they find it. When the shepherd loses his one sheep, he is willing to leave the ninety-nine others to search for this one because it is valued. Similarly, the woman is willing to search until she finds her one missing coin even though she has nine others because the one coin is valued. Likewise, if one dog was missing from a house, but they had nine others, the owner would still search because the one dog is valued. During the loss and searching, it can be scary, dangerous, and time-consuming. But it is all worth it because when the lost are found, there is joy. When just one person who was lost finds their way to Jesus, there is great joy. These parables remind us that Jesus is actively searching for us when we are lost, and there will be tremendous joy when we are found. This type of joy cannot be contained and cannot be celebrated alone. It can be expected that Jesus invites each of us to join all of heaven in celebrating when the lost are found. So whenever you feel lost or off-track, take comfort in knowing that Jesus will not give up on finding you because you are valued, and there will be great joy when you are found again.

In what ways are you currently off-track with your relationship with Jesus. What steps can you take to get back on-track?

_____

_____

_____

_____

_____

_____

_____

_____

_____

_____

A Lesson about Acceptance

This is Jesus' longest, and perhaps most famous, parable. Unique to Luke's gospel, the parable welcomes us into the inner conflict of family dynamics which often hits close to home.

Read Luke 15:11-32

Describe a time someone got credit for something even though you thought they didn't deserve it.

_____

_____

_____

In this parable, it may seem that the focus is on the two sons, but one could argue that the focus is actually on the father. Even though the younger son left and lost everything his father had given him, the father was still welcoming and excited for his return. The father did not chase after the son or try to find him, but he was waiting with open arms when he returned. Although the son did not feel worthy of being accepted back into the family, the father began planning a huge celebration. He completely accepted the son and was thrilled to have him back home. Despite the father's excitement, the older son was furious with the way his father acted and took it out through his feelings toward his brother. Sometimes we may resonate with the older brother's feelings. It can be common to be offended or hurt when someone else gets credit or is favored when you're annoyed with the person, or you aren't getting the same attention. We can sometimes have the same views about God's forgiveness and acceptance of others. It is not a competition or a position that only one person fills. Just because the younger son was welcomed and celebrated doesn't mean that the older son was rejected. The father went after the older son to remind him that he is still accepted and loved. We also need to be reminded that we are always important to God, and accepting someone else does not mean that we are rejected. After all, one day, we could be like the younger son and need God to be waiting with open arms ready to embrace and welcome us back, just like the father did.

Name a time that you felt rejected. Can you now understand the other side of the situation? Is it possible that the rejection you felt actually had to do with the other person?

_____

_____

_____

_____

_____

A Lesson about Humility

In what might be one of the most puzzling parables of Jesus, we come across a businessman who is cunning, devious, and possibly even corrupt. In several respects, the manager resembles us more than we would like to admit.

Read Luke 16:1-13

Have you ever worked for or with someone who was corrupt or misused things?

_____

_____

_____

Jesus' parable is about a man who manages a commercial enterprise dishonestly. It seems he is misappropriating some, or maybe a lot, of the money the business makes to pay for his own interests. Because he is embezzling, the owner fires him. Jesus tells us the manager is distraught and needs to hustle because he is too weak to work a labor-intensive job and too proud to beg. However, we have no lens into his feelings toward his dishonesty. For example, we can't discern if he's remorseful. Jesus tells us, though, that he quickly thinks of a new plan. This time the plan is less like embezzlement and more like a scheme. He's decided to entice those who owed his boss by cutting their bills. By reducing their debt, the owner lost profit. This is, after all, what got him fired. It's a puzzling parable because the owner actually praises this tactic. There are a few things we can learn from this parable. First, we run into problems when we misuse things such as money, power, or position. Second, the way we think about and use money, and the way wealth is accumulated is part of a broader and more dysfunctional system of abuses. And third, we are always connected to others. Although fired, the manager was in debt to the owner's grace. However, perhaps a fourth lesson may be found in this parable that is more subtle, yet more profound. A closer reading of verse four helps us realize that the manager's goal may not have been to squander his boss' money, but rather to seek the hospitality and support of others in a time of need. And so, perhaps, this is why he is praised.

The dishonest manager was afraid to beg, so instead he developed a scheme for others to help him. What's the difference? List ways you need to ask for help and ways you need to help others.

_____

_____

_____

_____

_____

A Lesson about Attention

It is unmistakable in Luke's gospel: God will bless the poor. However, a subversive part of this theme is that the wealthy have a responsibility to take care of the impoverished. Here we have a parable that further establishes this obligation.

Read Luke 16:19-31

Which character do you identify with in this parable? Why?

_____

_____

_____

The parable couldn't contrast two ways of life more vividly. First, there is a rich man, with presumably a fine gated house, wearing expensive clothes, and wasting time hanging out with lots of friends with a surplus of food. He was juxtaposed with a poor man, who presumably had been homeless and hungry for years and was also very ill. Lazarus, the poor man, was thrown at the rich man's gate. During this scene, the two actually don't meet. We are left to imagine that Lazarus succumbed to death by his condition of poverty. Worse, his body laid at the rich man's gate only to be licked by dogs. Because Lazarus wasn't even dignified with a proper burial, Jesus said the angels carried him to heaven. Before we can even suppose that poverty and richness is something just of this world, Jesus said the rich man also died. In his case, there wasn't an angelic procession to heaven, but instead, he was tormented in death. This, however, is not a theology of heaven and hell. This is a parable about the here and now. Jesus didn't live his entire life of solidarity with the poor, just for us to worry about ourselves. The rich man never even noticed Lazarus! It's repeated over and over. Luke can't describe the life and ministry of Jesus without revealing his ultimate attention to the poor. It's also safe to say, then, that a life of discipleship must be attentive to the needs of the poor.

If you haven't realized it, the author of Luke presumes that anyone educated enough to read his gospel is rich. Don't even worry about tying to imagine you are Lazarus. Imagine what you must do to change, if you were the rich man in this story.

_____

_____

_____

_____

_____

_____

_____

A Lesson about Persistence

In this parable, unique to Luke's gospel, a widow and a judge are highlighted. In the gospel, widows represent all who are disadvantaged, and judges represent all who know God's justice and the ethics of the Torah. Jesus' parable is comical and ironic, though, because the widow has high self-respect, and the judge is anything but just.

Read Luke 18:1-8

Name some characteristics of a widow.

_____

_____

Name some characteristics of a judge.

_____

_____

In this parable, a widow is relentless in her pursuit to get justice against her opponent. She continuously bothers and pushes back against the judge. We would hope that most judges would be fair, see each situation without bias, and do the right thing. This judge is quite the opposite. He didn't have respect for people, didn't fear God, and definitely didn't care about doing the right thing. This widow didn't care, though. She was going to keep boldly demanding justice until she got it even when it seemed like the situation wasn't going to change. Finally, the judge had enough and granted justice for the widow. He did this not because he wanted to do the right thing, but because he wanted the widow to stop pestering him. This parable ends by contrasting the judge and God. If the judge will reluctantly give someone what they need because they continuously beg him, imagine what God will do. If we call out to God, who truly wants what is best for us, his response would be different because he is not reluctant. However, we may still have to be relentless like the widow, because, as we know from reading Luke's gospel, our time may not line up with God's time. In the waiting, we can persevere through prayer and be confident that God willingly listens to and answers us.

When have you had to be persistent through prayer? Did God answer you, even if it wasn't as fast as you would have liked?

_____

_____

_____

_____

_____

_____

NOTES & JOURNALING

THE CALL OF JESUS

One might think in the two-thousand years of the Christian faith there would be a flood of examples of how demanding and costly the call of Jesus is. Unfortunately, that's simply not the case. Therefore, it's a great use of time to look at a few writers, like Dietrich Bonhoeffer, Dorothy Day, Martin Luther King, Jr., and others, to see first-hand the significance of Jesus' call. After reading Luke's gospel, we hope you too will realize that discipleship is demanding.

Too often, we think of Jesus' call to discipleship as merely believing. While belief plays a part, you will not see belief emphasized in Luke's gospel.

Instead, Jesus calls us to action, specifically to deny ourselves, take up our cross daily, and follow him. We can't forget, or set aside, that Jesus died on the cross. The cross is a symbol of death. There's no confusion, following Jesus include risks. Although we'd rather resist risks in our lives, Jesus' call is to deny ourselves and follow his example of a life of self-sacrifice, every single day.

Jesus calls each of us, and the Gospel of Luke doesn't hold back on the demands Jesus expects. The call of discipleship is costly. The cost of discipleship rings true when Jesus calls his first disciples and continues throughout the entirety of Luke's gospel. In one of the most famous stories in the Bible, we will see how much this costs Zacchaeus when he decides to give away half of his possessions. Although Jesus' demand for our lives is immense, his call comes with great benefit for all who follow.

Jesus' Call is Personal

The Bible refers to the Sea of Galilee and the Sea of Tiberius interchangeably. Luke is unique and calls it the Lake of Gennesaret after the town of the same name on the northwest shore. Much of Jesus' ministry was centered around this lake. At this point in Luke's gospel, Jesus encountered these empty-netted fishermen and hopped on one of their boats.

Read Luke 5:1-11

What are some things we already know about Jesus?

_____

_____

_____

It may seem odd for someone to hop into your boat (or car) without an invitation. Jesus wasn't just someone, he was already well known and even already had a crowd following him. He already had followers because he healed Simon's mother-in-law and others in the previous chapter. So, the fishermen already knew Jesus was a miracle worker, and after a day of no fish, maybe they were hoping for a miracle. Most of us already know some things about Jesus, and because of this, we have hopes of what Jesus may do in our lives. When Jesus hopped in Simon's boat, he told them to let down their nets, and they seemed to be reluctant. After all, Jesus wasn't a fisherman, and they had caught nothing all day. Yet, Simon still followed Jesus' instruction. We could learn from Simon to not let our own reluctance and self-will interfere with God's will. It was only after following Jesus that the nets overflowed with fish. That was the first miracle in this story. The second was Jesus' total redirection of their life. Instead of catching fish, he called them to catch people. He used the word catch because it made sense in the context of fishing. Jesus calls us to trust in him and redirect our lives so that we may follow him in ways that make sense to our own settings.

In what ways is Jesus calling you to redirect your life?

_____

_____

_____

_____

_____

_____

_____

_____

_____

_____

Jesus' Call is Inclusive

After Jesus called the disciples, he healed two men and then encountered Levi at the tax booth. Perhaps like today, there wasn't much love for tax collectors. However, Jesus was notorious for connecting with those less favored, like tax collectors, the poor, widows, and the sick.

Read Luke 5:27-32

Who are those less favored today?

_____

_____

_____

When Jesus saw Levi, he simply said to him, follow me. That's it: no conversation, no persuasive maneuvers, nor any special tactics. Jesus was direct and to the point. Levi equaled this call by leaving everything. Everything is an interesting word choice. Levi left everything. Think about this for a moment. Does this mean his job as a tax collector? His family? His money? His friends? What exactly does leaving everything mean? Luke doesn't answer these questions. All we know is that Levi got up, left everything, and followed him. But wait. Luke goes on to tell us that Levi hosted a great banquet for Jesus in his house. So Levi still had the means to give a banquet. He also apparently still had his home. Therefore, it's imperative for us to consider this word everything and what it could possibly mean. Conceivably, Levi left everything that could have distracted or prevented him from following Jesus. Maybe, Levi left everything in his life that was counter to Jesus' cause and message. Perhaps, God was already nudging Levi to reconsider his life, and Jesus' call to follow him was all he needed. So, Levi hosted a great banquet, with lots of people (who we would consider both favored and less favored) probably sitting at different sides of the table. It's important that everyone is invited to the banquet. Yet, Jesus made it clear that he is going to be at the side of those who need him most. Levi had a choice of who to sit with, and so do we.

Why is it important to pick a side of the table?

_____

_____

_____

_____

_____

_____

_____

_____

Jesus' Call is Uncomfortable

Jesus commissioned the disciples in Luke 9 and seventy more in Luke 10. These two commission stories are remarkably similar. In both stories, Jesus sent them out with little to no provisions, entirely dependent on what God provided.

Read Luke 9:1-6 and 10:1-12

To feel prepared, what are some things that are important to have with you?

_____

_____

_____

It would be foolish to show up to class unprepared. Everyone is different, but we each have things that we pack and bring to class to feel successful. Whether it is a laptop or phone charger, extra pencils, a water bottle, or a snack, we pack things just in case we need them. Similarly, we also prepare for trips. We often end up overpacking because we would rather be safe than sorry or want to have options. If you are packing for a summer beach trip, you might bring a jacket in case it is cold somewhere. If the forecast doesn't call for rain, you might still pack an umbrella just in case. We pack these extra things because we want to feel secure and prepared to handle any situation. Sometimes bringing one extra thing provides peace of mind instead of worrying about what to do if something unexpected happens that we didn't prepare for. When Jesus calls and sends us out as disciples, the mission isn't about us or the equipment we bring. It's not about having a peace of mind. Sure, it's a risk, but the call of discipleship involves trusting God's plan. Sometimes we will face rejection. When Jesus sent the seventy out, he warned of the risks of ministry to the wolves. While this is possible, it is also equally likely that we will be welcomed with open arms. When we show favor to others with a heart of love and acceptance as Jesus did, strangers will extend hospitality. If we had planned it alone with our equipment, we would not have the opportunity to experience their generosity and make a new friend.

Compare and contrast Luke's Commission vs Matthew 's (28:16-20).

Similarities	Differences

Jesus' Call is Challenging

This passage is divided into two sections. The first section deals with the identity of Jesus, and the second deals with Jesus' call for us to take up the cross. The identity of Jesus and the call of discipleship are directly related. In verse 20, Jesus asks, "who do you say that I am?" Peter had an answer. Eventually, every follower of Jesus must also answer this question.

Read Luke 9:18-27

Who do you say Jesus is? Peter said Jesus is the Messiah of God. What does being the Messiah of God mean to you?

_____

_____

_____

The call to follow Jesus is challenging (look at the introduction on page 70 for examples). However, Jesus never asked anyone to do anything he wasn't prepared to do himself. Verses 23-27 represent the core nature of discipleship in Luke's gospel. This section contains five sayings of Jesus. If anyone wants to be a follower of Jesus, they must first deny themselves and take up their cross daily. Jesus lived a life of self-denial that eventually led him to take up his cross. In the second saying, he confronts our need for self-preservation. Jesus, though, never lived for himself. Everything he did was for others. The third saying threatens our materialistic desires. Jesus lived in poverty, eating and staying with others, and dependent on the hospitality of strangers. The fourth saying questions our hesitations to be public with our faith. Yet, Jesus was very vocal that he was doing his Father's will. The fifth saying defies our belief that we will only see God's kingdom in Heaven. Jesus, however, reminds us that God's kingdom is right here among us. This path laid out, of following Jesus, is a road already traveled by Jesus. While the call to follow Jesus seems life-denying, it is actually life-giving. Following Jesus frees us from the constraints (arrogance, pride, greed, shame, fear, etc.) that burden our everyday life.

Let's break down two of the sayings in verses 23-27.

What it says	What it means to me
1. If any want to become my followers, let them, deny their cross daily and follow me.	
2. What does it profit them if they gain the whole world, but lose or forfeit themselves?	

Jesus' Call is Liberating

Jesus calls us not to worry. Although there are exceptions, a lot of times, we worry about things we can control. Jesus gives us insight on how to reduce our worries, at least when we are the source of our anxiety.

Read Luke 12:22-34

What are some things that you treasure?

_____

_____

_____

According to Jesus, the solution to worrying is having more trust in God. It appears from Jesus' stories that the ravens are worry-free because they obviously aren't constrained with worldly possessions. Yet, we are. We acquire and buy things that end up taking over our life. If we own a car, we have to take care of it, and when it breaks down, it costs a lot to repair. Being stuck in a life of having to buy new things not only weighs us down, it also corrodes our faith – leaving little room to trust God. Jesus also tells us that the lilies neither toil nor spin. This is a metaphor that could be paraphrased flowers aren't concerned with their appearance. Yet, we are. We spend time focusing on our appearance because it's what others see. It's easy to spend a lot of time getting ready, exercising, or dieting to get our appearance to match what we think is acceptable. We can spend even more time trying to take the perfect picture to post. The more time we spend on ourselves, the less time we have to devote to our faith – which again leaves little room to trust God. Both what we buy and the way we look consume us, and what consumes us is where we are invested. Jesus tells us, though, in verse 34, our treasure is where our heart is. So the solution to worrying is having more trust in God, or said another way, investing in God's call. Instead of buying so much, perhaps we can give more, and instead of spending so much time on ourselves, we can spend more of our time devoted to serving others.

How to spend my money better	How to spend my time better

Jesus' Call is Costly

In this section, Jesus calls us, bluntly, in three ways. First, discipleship must take precedence, even over our family life. Second, we are called to carry the cross. Finally, we can't be burdened by our possessions. This passage ends with Jesus telling us to listen.

Read Luke 14:25-35

Every new year people tend to make frivolous resolutions. What are some of the most trivial resolutions or commitments you have made?

_____

_____

_____

We are usually enthusiastic and excited the first week of class, and committed to making good grades. The same is true when we get a new job. During the first few weeks, we may strive to impress. When we first start dating someone, we are extra careful to be attentive and likable. Generally speaking, when we commit to something, we commit with good intentions and, therefore, always want to put our best foot forward. Committing to things like school, work, and healthy relationships should be valued. Sometimes we overcommit, and sometimes we commit to things that aren't valuable. We must ask ourselves, do our commitments cost more than we are willing to pay? At least that's what Jesus asked in these parables. Often we lose sight of our commitments. Slowly we begin to lack the motivation we initially had until we eventually aren't committed anymore. This process is usually gradual and hard to notice until it's too late. In verse 34, Jesus asked if salt has lost its taste, how can its saltiness be restored? Like commitments, salt loses its taste gradually, which is also hard to notice until it's too late. To keep salt good, we must preserve it. To keep our commitments, we must preserve them as well. Preserving our commitments takes dedication and persistence. This applies to both our everyday commitments and our commitment to the various calls of Jesus.

Hard commitments to keep	Ways to preserve them

Jesus' Call is Demanding

This is a story of a ruler in the community who approached Jesus on a spiritual quest. Luke tells us he had an abundance of wealth. Ironically, Jesus confronted his abundance and told him he actually lacked something.

Read Luke 18:18-30

What do you think the ruler was lacking?

_____

_____

_____

In chapter ten (in the parable of the good Samaritan), a lawyer asked Jesus what should he do to inherit eternal life. In this story, the rich ruler asked the same question. Both the lawyer and rich ruler seem to think eternal life is something you work for or earn. Eternal life is a question of salvation. Work we do is a question of discipleship. Discipleship is not a condition of salvation, but rather a response to it. Jesus saves, therefore we respond. The response Jesus wanted from the rich ruler was to sell everything. The thought of this made him sad. He must have liked being very rich. Perhaps he treasured his wealth more than having eternal life. Whatever the reason, he decided it was too costly to follow Jesus. He was right; following the call of Jesus' is demanding. It's easy to have our treasures become a barrier to following Jesus, but it's also easier to see this in others. It doesn't take much effort to read through this story and think the rich ruler made a mistake. It's much more challenging to realize that we are like the rich ruler. Most of us live far more abundantly than we would care to admit, and like the rich ruler, Jesus reminds us that we lack something as well. It's time for us to let go of the treasures in our lives that obstruct us from following Jesus.

What are some of your treasures and how can they sometimes be a barrier to following Jesus?

_____

_____

_____

_____

_____

_____

_____

_____

_____

_____

Jesus' Call is Transformational

A short man named Zacchaeus climbed a tree to get a better glimpse of Jesus when he entered the town of Jericho. Jesus favored the poor in the gospel, and Luke tells us Zacchaeus was a chief tax collector. This means Zacchaeus was not poor, but very wealthy and powerful.

Read Luke 19:1-10

Have you ever been on a spiritual retreat? If yes, what was your experience? If not, what do you think it entails?

_____

_____

_____

Most places in Israel and Palestine (the Holy Land) are barren and desert-like. Jericho is in the West Bank, so many pilgrims (anyone on a spiritual journey) to the Holy Land avoid Jericho and therefore miss how fertile and lush the city is. That day in Jericho, Zacchaeus was a pilgrim because he wanted to see Jesus. Most of us have had times where we wanted to be closer to God. We may be working through this devotional to get a better view of Jesus. We read the scriptures and go to worship to get a closer glimpse of God. We can relate to Zacchaeus, in so many ways. Then Luke tells us that Jesus looked up to Zacchaeus and acknowledged him. Zacchaeus' goal was to see Jesus, but instead, Jesus saw him. That's what happens: when we seek God, God seeks us. Without a call, Zacchaeus willingly started the path of discipleship by giving to the poor and paying back those he cheated. As a result, Jesus told him salvation had come to his house. A true transforming and conversion-like experience was happening, without any religious or spiritual talk. Zacchaeus realized that following Jesus had less to do with words, and more to do with him righting his wrongs.

Zacchaeus' efforts to get closer to God ended in a promise. Scholars believe the verbs in his promise are present progressive, meaning that Zacchaeus intended to continually give to the poor and continually right his wrongs. What are steps you can take now, that you will continue in the future, to get closer to God?

_____

_____

_____

_____

_____

_____

_____

Jesus' Call is Indispensable

Throughout chapters 20 and 21, Jesus taught in the temple, warning the religious leaders of their piety and lack of faith. He also told how a widow placed two coins into the temple's offering. She put in all that she had.

Read Luke 21:1-4

What stands out to you from this passage?

_____

_____

_____

Throughout Luke's gospel, Jesus had a problem with the religious leaders. The temple system was, quite frankly, corrupt, and Jesus always responded sharply to their criticism, practices, and lifestyle. One example of their behavior was to convince even the most destitute and most impoverished people to give to the system's treasury. This widow offered the temple all she had. It's ironic that just a few years later, the temple was destroyed. There are countless examples of how elite people benefit at the expense of those who are poor. Sometimes they even get praised for how significantly large their gifts are. Maybe Jesus' didn't praise her, but he certainly highlighted the widow's gift instead. He reminded that the rich gave out of abundance, and she gave out of poverty. The offering the rich gave was dispensable income, like play money. Everything the widow owned was indispensable. For Jesus, it's not about the amount you give, but about the amount that remains after giving. The rich people walked away with plenty while she walked away with nothing. The kingdom of God is never symbolized by how much we have or how much we give. The kingdom of God isn't represented by elite religious leaders or the prideful rich. God's kingdom is exemplified by a poor widow.

How are we called to be like the widow, who exemplified God's kingdom?

_____

_____

_____

_____

_____

_____

_____

_____

_____

_____

_____

Jesus' Call is Irrevocable

Jesus entered Jerusalem for the last time, only to be betrayed and arrested. As they brought Jesus to the high priest for trial, Peter followed at a distance. On three separate occasions, people accused Peter of being a follower or friend of Jesus. Each time Peter denied this.

Read Luke 22:54-62

We all mess up. Name a time or two when you've messed up.

_____

_____

_____

No one in Luke's gospel was closer to Jesus than Peter. He was the first disciple to be called and accompanied Jesus to the end (at least from afar). Before this section, Peter told Jesus he was ready to go with him to prison and even to death. It's fair to say Peter was all in. It looks like Peter had mapped it out and planned out the way he hoped to follow Jesus. However, he didn't follow through with his intentions, broke his promise to Jesus, and lied about even knowing him. Luke tells us that Peter wept bitterly when Jesus looked at him. Peter was crushed. Peter knew he failed. He was devastated by himself. Often, we beat ourselves up as well. When things go wrong in a relationship, we can be harsh on ourselves. When we feel separated from our faith, we blame ourselves. Our own self-pity can become a crutch. We can use it against ourselves unknowingly by saying things like "I'm bad at relationships," or "I'm not good enough for church." Our attempt to be unpretentious can become annoyingly pretentious. It's irritating mostly because it is self-centered. Peter messed up, and so in self-pity, he wept. But Peter wasn't a failure. After all, he was the only disciple who even risked being near Jesus at the end. He also goes on to lead God's people in the Book of Acts. Jesus' call is simply irrevocable. Jesus not only forgives us, but he also calls us to forgive ourselves, move on, and be God's work and presence in the world.

When I've self-doubted	How I used it as a crutch	How I will move forward

Notes & Journaling

_____

_____

_____

_____

_____

_____

_____

_____

_____

_____

_____

_____

_____

_____

_____

_____

_____

_____

_____

_____

Luke develops several themes in his account of the life and ministry of Jesus. First, Jesus' Jewish homeland was occupied by the Roman Empire. Luke is careful not to demonize Rome's authoritarian role. Instead, Luke focuses on the perversion of the religious system. Jesus disrupts current religious behavior through two more significant themes. One is Jesus' call of repentance and forgiveness of sins. The other is Jesus' dedication to the Father, especially through prayer. Five additional themes highlight Luke's gospel. They are addressed here.

About Simon Peter

Simon Peter was one of Jesus' twelve disciples. He was a fisherman from Galilee and is prominent in all four gospels and the book of Acts. In Matthew, Mark, and John, Simon was called by Jesus and given a new name, *Petra*. *Petra* means rock in Greek. In Aramaic, the language Jesus spoke, the word for rock is *Cepha*. Therefore, he is referred to as *Cephas* in John's gospel and other New Testament writings. In Luke, he is referred to interchangeably as Simon, Simon Peter, and Peter. Interestingly, in Luke's gospel, there is no mention of the special naming of Simon. Subtly in Luke 5, the author started to call Simon, Simon Peter. In chapter six, though, Luke does say Jesus named Simon with the new name of Peter. In Mark, Peter was presented less favorably, though most thoroughly. Peter was certainly not beloved disciple in John. In Matthew, Jesus says, built his church on this rock, meaning Peter. Thus, Roman Catholics have ever since considered Peter the first Pope. However, it appears that Peter was Jesus' closest disciple in Luke's gospel and even had a unique appearance with the resurrected Jesus in Luke 24:34. After Jesus' ascension, Peter took on a significant leadership role in the book of Acts, also written by Luke.

SCRIPTURE REFERENCES: Luke 5:1-11; 6:12-16; 9:18-20

About Food in Luke's Gospel

"In Luke's Gospel Jesus is either going to a meal, at a meal, or coming from a meal."[4] In every single chapter of Luke's gospel, food, or the thought of food is mentioned. Jesus ate with Levi, Simon the Pharisee, Martha, and Zacchaeus. He fed five thousand by the lake, broke bread at the Passover, and was called a glutton, drunkard, and friend of sinners. It was at the table where Jesus confronted his followers and foes together, breaking social barriers and exemplifying the necessity of hospitality, especially to the stranger, outcast, and excluded. The copious mentions of food stress Luke's concern with hunger. Hunger isn't spiritualized in Luke's gospel. Jesus understands the actual lack of access to nourishment, especially to those who are poor. Thus, Jesus was the Messiah who Mary prophesied would literally fill the hungry with good things and send the rich away empty. The fact that impoverished people worldwide remain hungry in the twenty-first century reveals the significance of Jesus' message and ministry right now. We must continue to use food to feed those in need and bring people together through the hospitality of sharing.

SCRIPTURE REFERENCES: Luke 5:27-32; 9:10-17; 22:14-38

---

[4] Robert J. Karris, Eating Your Way through Luke's Gospel. Order of Saint Benedict, 2006), 97.

About The New Exodus

The Gospel of Luke draws heavily on the Hebrew Bible, and particularly the Exodus, the most foundational story in the Old Testament. Moses, the protagonist of the Exodus narrative, led the Israelites from the oppressive empire to the land of freedom. Luke focuses on Jesus' radical message of liberation to lead God's people out of a new oppressive regime. Unlike Moses, Jesus had to deal with the oppressive Roman Empire and the authoritarian religious leaders who controlled the temple. Jesus was leading a new, or second Exodus. Moses and Elijah appeared with Jesus at his transfiguration and even talked about his departure to Jerusalem. The Greek word for departure is *exodos*. Like Moses, who wandered for forty years in the wilderness, Jesus was tested for forty days in the wilderness. Like Moses, who rescued the people from the raging waters, Jesus calmed the violent sea. Just as Moses proclaimed the Torah, Jesus preached long discourses on the ways of the Father. As Moses fed the Israelites, Jesus fed five thousand. However, unlike Moses, who died, Jesus' death was overcome by his victory with the resurrection.

SCRIPTURE REFERENCES: Luke 4:1-13; 8:22–25; 9:28-36

About The Great Reversal

If Jesus is the protagonist in Luke's gospel, the poor are his love interest. More explicitly, the poor are God's love interest. For Luke, the poor includes all on the fringe of society who are neglected, mistreated, overlooked, oppressed, and abused. Typically, the poor are presented as economically impoverished, sick, hungry, or outcast because of various impurities imposed by the rich. The rich refers to those who are comfortable, who already have status, seem to have enough physical resources, perhaps have religious authority, and most importantly for Luke's gospel, reject Jesus. It would be one thing if the rich rejected Jesus just because he loved the poor, but they rejected Jesus because he proclaimed that in God's kingdom, their roles will reverse, hence the great reversal. In the sermon on the plain, Jesus said the poor are the ones God blesses. It is easy to see Jesus as a spiritual guide or a savior who redeems us. Yet, Jesus brought about a social revolution. Jesus wasn't just preaching for the reversal; he was embodying the reversal as a homeless and rejected prophet, calling his disciples to follow him empty-handed, and demanding that the rich sell all of their possessions. To be committed to God's kingdom, Jesus tells us we must be relentlessly committed to the care of the poor. Period.

SCRIPTURE REFERENCES: Luke 6:17-49; 12:22-34; 16:19-31

About The Lukan Triangle

All four gospels have central characters, such as Jesus, the disciples, religious leaders (such as Pharisees or scribes), and participants of Jesus' healings and signs. All four gospels also mention that Jesus drew large crowds. However, this multitude, called the crowd, plays different roles in each of the gospels. Most encounters in Luke highlight Jesus, a main character, and someone from a crowd. Often, it's a member of the crowd that presents a challenge for Jesus. Brendan Byrne, an Australian Biblical scholar, calls this trio of characters The Lukan Triangle. The trouble-making crowd members were usually judgmental or hypocritical. They were finger-pointers and fault-finders. They smirked, probably rolled their eyes, most certainly talked behind Jesus' back, and outright opposed him in a covert manner. Their resistance, though, wasn't limited just to Jesus. They also were the chief instigators in calling attention to or labeling other's troubles. They overtly called people sinners, for example. The Lukan Triangle exposes Luke's keen sense of the human condition and the toxicity of judgmental behavior. As a composite, these members of the crowd epitomized everything a disciple should avoid: being self-centered, unkind, and manipulative, lacking empathy, and gossiping. We will always have critics in our lives, but we can't let them get the best of us.

SCRIPTURE REFERENCES: Luke 5:22-39; 6:1-5; 19:1-10

Notes & Journaling

Suggested Readings

Byrne, Brendan. *The Hospitality of God: A Reading of Luke's Gospel*. Liturgical Press, 2015.

Carroll, John T. *Luke: A Commentary*. Westminster John Knox Press, 2012.

Craddock, Fred B. *Luke: Interpretation: A Bible Commentary for Teaching and Preaching*. John Knox Press, 1990.

Culpepper, R. Alan. *The Gospel of Luke. The New Interpreter's Bible*: Volume 9. Abingdon Press, 1995.

Fitzmyer, Joseph A. *Luke 1-9: Introduction, Translation, and Notes*. Doubleday, 1981.

––––––. *Luke 10-24: Introduction, Translation, and Notes*. Doubleday, 1981.

Gonzàllez, Justo L. *Luke*. Westminster John Knox Press, 2010.

Green, Joel B. *The Gospel of Luke. The New International Commentary on the New Testament*. Grand Rapids, Mich: W.B. Eerdmans Pub. Co, 1997.

Jarvis, Cynthia A. and E. Elizabeth Johnson, ed. *Feasting on the Gospels-Luke* (Vol.1): A Feasting on the Word Commentary. Westminster John Knox, 2014.

––––––. *Feasting on the Gospels-Luke* (Vol.2): A Feasting on the Word Commentary. Westminster John Knox, 2014.

Johnson, Luke Timothy. *The Gospel of Luke*. Liturgical Press, 2006.

Karris, Robert J. *Eating Your Way through Luke's Gospel*. Order of Saint Benedict, 2006.

Newsom, Carol A., Sharon H. Ringe, and Jacqueline E. Lapsley. *Women's Bible Commentary: Revised and Updated*. Westminster John Knox Press, 2012.

Ringe, Sharon H. *Luke*. Westminster John Knox Press, 1995.

Schweizer, Eduard. *The Good News According to Luke*. John Knox Press, 1984.

Tannehill, Robert C. *Luke*. Abingdon Press, 1996.

Voris, Steven J. *Preaching Parables: A Metaphorical Interfaith Approach*. Paulist Press, 2008.

Index

Luke 2:1-21	6	Luke 14:1-14	66
Luke 3:21-22	8	Luke 14:25-35	94
Luke 4:1-13	10	Luke 15:1-10	68
Luke 4:16-30	12	Luke 15:11-32	70
Luke 5:1-11	84	Luke 16:1-13	72
Luke 5:27-32	86	Luke 16:19-31	74
Luke 6:20-36	58	Luke 17:11-19	44
Luke 6:37-49	60	Luke 18:1-8	76
Luke 7:11-17	32	Luke 18:18-30	96
Luke 7:36-50	34	Luke 19:1-10	98
Luke 8:22-25	36	Luke 19:28-40	16
Luke 8:40-56	38	Luke 21:1-4	100
Luke 9:1-6	88	Luke 22:14-23	46
Luke 9:10-17	40	Luke 22:39-46	48
Luke 9:18-27	90	Luke 22:47-53	18
Luke 9:28-36	14	Luke 22:54-62	102
Luke 10:1-12	88	Luke 23:26-49	20
Luke 10:25-42	62	Luke 24:1-12	22
Luke 11:1-13	64	Luke 24:13-35	50
Luke 12:22-34	92	Luke 24:50-53	24
Luke 13:10-17	42